HIT THE GROUND RUNNING

How Start-ups Can Start Right

By

Dr. Ukadike Ake

© Copyright 2020 by Ukadike Ake – All rights reserved.

It is not legal to reproduce, duplicate or transmit any part of this document in either electronic means or printed format. Recording of this publication is strictly prohibited.

This book is dedicated to:

To my gang. My wonderful wife, partner and friend Siya and our lovely children, you guys feed me energy.

Table of Contents

Introduction 1

Chapter One - Getting Back to the Basics: The Case for Planning... 4

Chapter Two - Is It Really Worth It? Economic Viability of Your Venture 19

Chapter Three - Feeding the Wolf: Getting Funds for Your Business 34

Chapter Four – Setting Up Your Structure 44

Chapter Five - What Comes Through the Door: Recruiting in Small Businesses….....................................50

Bibliography 59

Appendix - Sample Business Plan.. 61

Acknowledgements 85

About the Author 92

Introduction

This book is written for people who intend to start a small business or who have already started one. A lot of people have wonderful ideas on the business venture they want to start, and some are even skilled in one area or the other, but they have no idea on how to go about setting up a business structure that harnesses their skills and ideas. This book provides a stepwise plan of action to starting your business. In addition, the concepts and arguments presented in this book, are expressed in plain and non-technical language, so that anyone can benefit from them.

This book attempts to help the entrepreneur avoid failures inherent in starting up a new business. These pitfalls are there because there is a dearth of the basic knowledge on factors and processes entrepreneurs need to grasp to start a successful venture. For instance, starting a venture without planning is one recipe for failure because this means the business has no scope and no research has been carried out about the internal and external environments the owner/drivers intend to operate within. This book will help you to understand how to plan. It also presents other vital areas for start-ups, such as seeking for funds and recruiting.

I have had several personal experiences with these types of failures I talk about in this book. I was a teenager when I started my first venture with my brothers. We set up a pool (snooker) board in front of the family house and charged our friends for each round of 8-ball pool. Since, then I have undertaken one venture after another and now I find myself in the hospitality/real estate sectors. My entrepreneurial sojourn has spanned over 25 years with a lot of mistakes, exactly the kinds of mistakes I try to get others to avoid in this book.

I spent a lot of time in the classroom studying about businesses and management because I wanted to succeed in business and also to help others thrive. I hold an MBA and a Doctorate degree in Business Administration, and I believe the combination of practical experience and academic knowledge gives me an insight to the intricacies and peculiarities of business organizations and entrepreneurship.

This book is the first in a series designed for small business start-ups. This book will help the entrepreneur understand areas that they might ordinarily need to rely on 'experts' to work on. After reading this book, the business starter will be able to decide if the venture, he or she wants to undertake is worth it. The reader will understand the importance of the organizational structure and why she should not just adopt what everyone is doing. What is more, the reader will have clarity going into the processes of hiring new employees and sourcing for funds for the business.

Venturing into business, for many, is like diving into the deep unknown, especially when considering that you are putting at stake your savings and future. But you can't succeed if you do not start. Learning about starting a business gives you an edge by making the process less murky and this book shines the light on some of the often confusing and cloudy areas. Now come with me and let's get started.

Hit the Ground Running

Chapter One - Getting Back to Basics: The Case for Planning

Hit the Ground Running

I started writing articles on small businesses and management as an experiment. I wanted to reflect on all I was doing wrong, as a small businessperson myself, by writing about how to do it right. It is important, that the entrepreneur gets it right from the beginning – you have to start by planning. Remember, Eddy Murphy quoting Friedrich Nietzsche in the movie, 'Coming to America' - *"He who would learn to fly one day must first learn to walk and run and climb and dance; one cannot fly into flying."* Planning is like learning to walk but dreaming of flying.

There's that popular story about a man given 10 hours or so to cut a tree and he decides to spend 8 hours sharpening his axe and this captures the importance of planning. Planning gives you a better chance as success because it helps you avoid some pitfalls that lie in wait in the future and also helps you think more about the nitty-gritty and external factors of the business you intend going into.

Why Should We Plan?

    The way I see it, if you have unlimited resources to put into your start-up, then you don't need to plan. Best case, you get others to plan for you. But if your resources are not bountiful (that's why it's a small

Hit the Ground Running

business, stupid), you have to plan, and this has to be done by you, the business owner, for several reasons. Firstly, no one is (or should be) more intimate with the business than you. For a lot of people, this is what they have dreamed of for a long time and so they have had a lot of time to think about it. Even if this is not the case for you, the venture you're thinking of going into will be a significant part of your future, as you will put in a lot of time and money into it and it will affect your future financial status.

In case you haven't guessed it, I've been talking about writing a business plan. I can just see a lot of guys cringing, yeah, I know, most people detest writing business plans, but doing this is a critical part of succeeding in your business. Like I said, you don't have inordinate resources, hence, it might be too expensive learning through avoidable mistakes. Writing a business plan helps you identify the risks and potential avoidable mistakes involved in the project before you commence, it also opens your eyes to the size (financially, mentally and physically) of what you're getting into.

Hit the Ground Running

This book is about making it simple for the intending 'starter-upper', hence, I have no intention to complicate any of the concepts. I have included a sample business plan in this book (Appendix section), to be used as a reference to articulate your own peculiar project.

Consequences of Not Planning

There are some situations, where opportunities just appear that you have to take advantage of, and you might not have time to write a business plan before you start. However, it is still important to go back and articulate a plan, even whilst the business venture has started operations. I was once involved in such a venture, where my partner and I had to take advantage of an opening that popped up suddenly. We had the opportunity to provide, on lease, construction equipment for a client on a running basis and this is how we got into the heavy equipment leasing sector. Throughout our foray into this scene, we failed to put down a plan and this had several disadvantages. Firstly, we failed to

Hit the Ground Running

define the scope of our operations. We started with earth-moving equipment (pay loaders and bulldozers) and veered into tipper trucks, which we probably wouldn't have if we took time to craft a plan that defined our target market. Secondly, we didn't do any initial analysis of our expected expenses and this dogged us for a while, because we kept spending a lot on 'unexpected' maintenance. If we had done our research from the beginning, we would have had a guide to the figures expected for issues such as maintenance and other operational expenses.

Our failure to plan, also meant we were blind to other vital areas of attention for the business, such as taxes. It was only when taxes were due, we became aware of the amounts we were due to pay and the kinds of taxes we had to pay.

What is a Business Plan?

A business plan is a document that articulates what the drivers of the business project intend to undertake and how they plan to go about executing. The plan provides a glimpse of the current environment their product will be going into, the problem they intend to resolve and how their skills and resources will make their idea a success. The business plan allows you to break down your vision into smaller tasks and this makes the project seem more manageable and achievable. Writing a plan for your business gets you thinking and researching into areas that you might likewise take for granted or not even think about. Areas like the size of your target market, details of your competitors, as well as marketing and sales strategies. Ultimately, the process of putting a plan to paper (or digital screen) helps you to know a lot more about your business than you would, if you did not go through this process.

The kind of plan I'm talking about at this stage does not have to be complex. At this stage, this plan is basically for you, the business owner. It could be more complex if you have to present it to your bankers or other financiers. Then you could bring in external help if you choose to, but what you have done initially, will serve as the basis of any bigger plan or presentation. Also, you can easily talk about it and sell the plan, since at its core, you are the author.

What's in a Business Plan?

The basic plan should contain several sections including a summary of the business itself: what it is all about, what problems it aims to solve, what are the product offerings etc. The plan should also contain a market summary, which delves into areas such as the size of the overall market, the target market, the competitors and the marketing strategy. Moreover, the plan should look into the financials of the project, these include the capital and operational expenses, the price strategy, the cash flow analysis, profit analysis and the break-even period. In addition, you should at this stage carry out a form of risk analysis, the most common is the SWOT (strengths, weaknesses, opportunities and threats) analysis.

The business plan should articulate the problem you are trying to solve. As the saying goes, *"where there is a problem, lies an opportunity"*. In most situations, you will find out that the problem is not a novel one and others are also providing solutions, but it is possible that you intend to provide a unique approach to serving the needs or the providers aren't simply adequate for the demand.

Hit the Ground Running

Management Plan

The plan could include the management setup/plan. For instance, who the key players are and the experiences and skills they bring on board. This section could also provide the structure of the organization and present the roles to handle the key responsibilities. This demonstrates one of the benefits of writing a plan, as it gets you thinking farther down the road. It pushes the entrepreneur to focus not only on the grand strategies and vision but also on bare-knuckle tactics that will get the project afloat and moving.

Marketing Plan

Hit the Ground Running

The business plan should as well present the marketing plan. This section of the plan should cover information on the target market – the geography of the target market, the trends and growth that have been occurring as regards to this market. This section should also articulate the possible competitors (both direct and indirect) and the pricing strategy you intend to adopt. It will be very likely that the person just venturing into business will have no clue on some of these issues and that is another advantage of the business plan, it forces you to carry out your research. If your business is to succeed, you have to know the terrain you are going into and you need to have a firm grasp on marketing tactics you want to deploy to ensure your product gets to its intended customers.

Financial Plan

In addition, the plan should provide the financial analysis you have carried out. I talk more about financial evaluation in the next chapter because this could determine if you should invest your resources or not. Let's face it, unless it is a charity effort, if the economics of the venture are not promising, it won't be worth it to even start in the first place. This area helps you to avoid failure in the future and this will be what most financiers will be looking out for. The next chapter also helps in explaining some of the concepts/tools needed in producing a financial analysis of the project/venture.

Risk Assessment

As mentioned earlier, it might also be a good idea to carry out a risk analysis at this point. Several analysis techniques exist but to keep it simple I would just recommend a SWOT analysis. SWOT stands for strengths, weaknesses, opportunities and threats. Strengths and weaknesses should focus on internal factors to the business such as the presence or lack of specialized skills. While, opportunities and threats should focus on factors external to the business such as new government policies or even a global health pandemic.

As promised, I don't intend to delve into any technical jargon, what I would advise is to look at the sample plan provided in the Appendix section and using the headings, write about your own business. Yours must not be as voluminous or detailed as the sample plan especially in the initial phase but you can see this as a work in progress, a document that you can always come back to update.

Chapter summary/Key takeaways

- Writing a business plan helps you break your project into smaller tasks that makes the project seem more manageable and achievable. It also helps avoid future failures and nudges the

entrepreneur to carry out vital research on the venture.
- The plan should include a presentation on the problems the business intends to solve and the opportunities these provide.
- The management plan expresses the skills and strengths the key players bring to table and also the management structure of the new organization.
- The marketing plan documents the target market's characteristics, information on competition and the pricing strategy.
- The financial plan analyzes the economic viability of the business venture.
- The risk analysis identifies potential threats and dangers that could confront the entrepreneur when venturing into the project.

Hit the Ground Running

The next chapter will talk about deciding if it's really worth going into the particular business venture you've chosen. We decide this using some basic tools that anyone can understand without paying a professional. Trust me, you'll see.

Chapter Two - Is It Really Worth It?
Economic Viability of Your Venture

Hit the Ground Running

Hopefully, the process of writing a business plan brings more clarity to the clutter of big plans flying around in your head and you are able to list out your product offerings i.e. what products or services you intend to sell and the process also helps you understand your environment better.

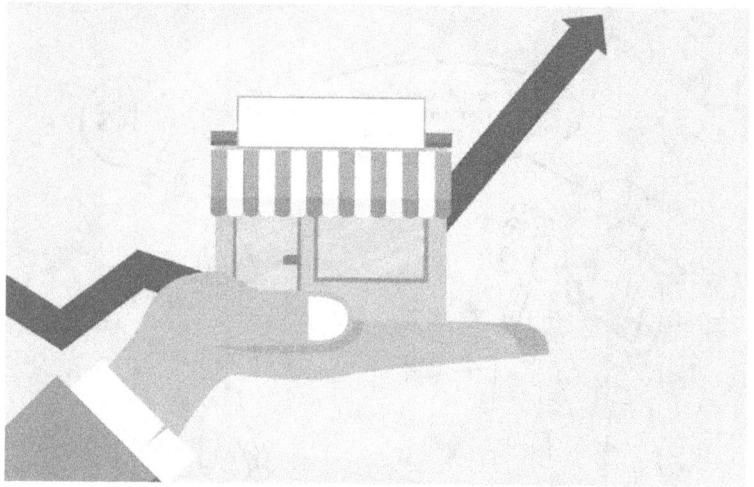

The next thing is to analyze the viability of the venture, how profitable will this idea turn out to be and how long will it take to break even. This analysis could also make up the business or marketing plan you intend to present to potential investors or will serve for your personal planning. Investors are always impressed when

Hit the Ground Running

you present an analysis of the proposed venture, it demonstrates thoroughness on your part. In the past, I have carried out an analysis on a real estate development I planned to undertake and from the output of my analysis, I decided to shelve the project. Some ventures end up not looking as rosy as they seemed, when the numbers are crunched and presented in black and white.

Now, don't start getting scared. In this chapter, we will not get too complex. We will leave the complex analyses for the accountants and finance guys. We will just look at the basics of how to evaluate your business and make decisions. Besides, this is the only chapter in this book, I talk about any form of computation and if it gets too confusing, you can always move to the next chapter and come back gradually, little steps at a time.

Hit the Ground Running

Identifying the Outflows and Inflows

Firstly, you will need to identify your capital expenditure (CAPEX) and put figures to these items. These are the costs expended in acquiring fixed assets such as land, buildings, equipment etc. So, if you intend to open a hair salon, your capital investments will include the hair dryers and other styling equipment, furniture, generator etc. These costs are not recurrent like rent and salaries, and these are usually spread over a period, for example 12 months, 3 years and so on and so forth.

Moving along, we then identify our operational expenditure (OPEX) and quantify them over a period of time, a year for example. These operational costs are the recurrent, day to day or month to month expenses, such as rent, salaries and wages, fuel and other consumables for the business. So, using our hair salon example, our operational costs should include the dyes, hair conditioners, other hair products used on clients, electricity costs, rent, salaries etc.

Hit the Ground Running

The next item to analyze should be the expected revenues. This is done by multiplying our unit price by the expected sales for any given period. A note of caution here, you should try to be as conservative as possible. For our salon business, we shouldn't plan on a full house for the first few months of the business. If you are starting up a guest house business, you shouldn't expect that you would have 100% or even 80% occupancy at the start of operations. Rather, it might be safer to plan with 20% or 30% occupancy in the initial stages, it is even smart to go lower for the first few months. So, for a given period (like a year), we should analyze our expected revenues, just as we have done for our capital and operational expenditures.

We will then take away our taxes and expenses from our revenues and this gives us our cash-flow for the given period.

Hit the Ground Running

Conducting the Economic Analysis

Below I present an example using an imaginary product, let's go with widgets. The table below captures the analysis for the first five years (year 0 to year 4) of the company called XYZ Widget Masters Limited. Initially, the price of the product is N500 and is gradually increased to N700 over three years and remains the same for the next two years, but the units-sold sees increases over the years and this also affects the revenues. The capital expenditure (CAPEX) is spread over the first two years of operation, while the operational costs (OPEX) are recurring year on year.

Hit the Ground Running

YEAR	UNIT PRICE (N)	UNITS SOLD (N)	REVENUE (N)	TAXES (N)	CAPITAL EXPENDITURE (N)	OPERATIONAL EXPENDITURE (N)	CASH FLOW (N)	DISCOUNTED CASH FLOW (12%)
0	500	480	240,000.00	72,000.00	1,000,000.00	50,000.00	(882,000.00)	(882,000.00)
1	600	720	432,000.00	129,600.00	500,000.00	60,000.00	(257,600.00)	(230,000.00)
2	700	960	672,000.00	201,600.00	-	65,000.00	405,400.00	323,182.40
3	700	1200	840,000.00	252,000.00	-	65,000.00	523,000.00	372,261.07
4	700	1200	840,000.00	252,000.00	-	65,000.00	523,000.00	332,375.96
TOTAL	3200	4560	3,024,000.00	907,200.00	1,500,000.00	305,000.00	311,800.00	(84,180.58)
					TOTAL EXPENDITURE	1,805,000.00		

NPV @12%	(84,180.58)
IRR	9%
PVR	-5%
ROI	68%

Hit the Ground Running

TABLE 1: ECONOMIC VIABILITY ANALYSIS OF XYZ WIDGET MASTERS LTD.

The cash flow is gotten by deducting the costs (Taxes + CAPEX + OPEX) from the revenue, which is negative in XYZ's first two years of operation as can be seen from the table. I know I promised not to get too complex, but I have added a few items that might be new to the non-finance people reading this but do not despair, as these concepts are fairly straightforward.

In order for us to decide if the investment is worthwhile, we need to apply some tools to help us make sound judgments.

Discounting refers to the conversion of future cash flow to a present value, thus, the term discounted cash flow. See formula below for **Discounted Cash Flow (DCF)**, it is the reverse of the compound interest formula:

$$PV = CF/(1+i)^n.$$

Where,

i = discounted rate.

CF = Cash flow at a point in time n.

PV = Present value of Cash Flow or cash flow in year 0.

n = the period of time between PV and CF expressed in years.

The discount rate is a matter of decision by the company or individual investing. The discount rate should consider the company's desired rate of growth and also future or alternative investment opportunities and possibly their relative risks.

Some companies assign a figure greater than the weighted cost of capital from all sources, while others use the minimum acceptable rate of return on investments. Some companies, in a bid to allow for uncertainties and risks, use very high discount rates. This decreases the risk of making a bad decision but increases the risk of turning down a worthwhile investment

Hit the Ground Running

opportunity. Since there is hardly any agreement on the choice of the correct discount rate, it is also advisable to use a range of discount rates in order to show the effects of this factor on the present value of cash flow[1].

In our example, we use a discount rate of 12% just for demonstration sakes, to get our discounted cash flow (or present value) figures for each year. For example, the first year we get our DCF (present value) by using the formula above:

$$PV \text{ (for year 0)} = -882,000/(1+0.12)^0$$

$$= -882,000/(1.12^0) = -882,000/1$$

$$= -882,000.$$

The value of i (1, 2, 3, 4) changes the DCF for the subsequent years.

The **Net Present Value (NPV)** is the first decision tool we consider. The NPV converts the future cash flow for an investment opportunity into an equivalent value at a particular point in time, the present (year 0). The sum of all present values of the discounted cash flows give the NPV. As can be seen from Table 1, the NPV is the sum of the discounted cash flows from years 0 to 4.

A positive NPV indicates the maximum amount that we can pay for an investment and still get our minimum acceptable rate of return. It also indicates how much could be invested in the project and not lose money. From our example in Table 1, we get a negative NPV (-84,180.58), which indicates the investment yielded a loss after the five-year period.

We will now look at three other decision criteria used in the example.

The **Present Value Ratio (PVR)** measures the NPV of a project and compares it to the initial investment. Unlike

NPV, PVR considers the magnitude of the initial investment in its assessment of profitability. By measuring profitability per currency (Naira or Dollar) invested, PVR allows us to rank both large and small projects according to profitability.

$$PVR = NPV/\text{Initial investment}.$$

From our example, we obtain a PVR of -5%, which is less than our discounted rate. This implies that the investment would yield less than our cost of finance or the minimum acceptable rate of return.

The **Internal Rate of Return (IRR)** is the average percentage return that an investment is expected to yield over its lifetime. This represents the highest cost of capital which would be incurred to raise funds for and investment without suffering economic loss. Unlike the previous two investment decision criteria, the IRR does not require selecting a discount rate. Microsoft Excel has a formula for calculating the IRR, so you don't have to manually do this. Just type =IRR (the cash flow range), then Excel does the rest. In our example we get an IRR of 9%, which can be interpreted as the average rate the investment is expected to return over its duration.

Lastly, we look at a commonly used investment decision tool used by marketing executives, the **Return on Investment (ROI)**. This is a ratio between the net profit over a period of time and the cost of investment. From our example, we obtain a return on investment of 68%, which is quite high but if we put this alongside our other tools (NPV, PVR and IRR), this investment actually rates poorly. We can see that we have negative values for NPV and PVR, as well as a very low IRR value, this tells us that the ROI figure can be very deceptive.

The example and tools presented above are intended to provide you with the right weapons to analyze that big idea you can't wait to get started on, before your dreams bring you despair. Hopefully, you don't make the same mistakes many others (including yours truly) have made by jumping in headfirst without carrying out any form of economic analysis. One more point from our example, we can observe that it takes two years to getting out more money than what has been spent and this is common in most businesses, often it takes even longer. The entrepreneur should be realistic and ready to be patient, which is not the case for most, who have dreams of instant cash outs.

Chapter summary/Key takeaways

- Analyzing the economic viability of your venture helps you decide if it's worth going into.
- Identify your expenditure, which would include your capital and operational costs.
- Then identify your potential revenues over a chosen period of time.

- The calculation of your cash flows and discounted cash flows provides figures for your decision-making analyses.
- Decision-making tools include Net Present Value (NPV), Present Value (PV), Internal Rate of Return (IRR) and Return on Investment (ROI). These will allow you to decide how viable the venture could turn out to be.

In the next chapter, we will talk about the fuel for every business venture, funding. We discuss the various sources of funds and the options every entrepreneur can explore to finance their business.

Chapter Three - Feeding the Wolf: Getting Funds for Your Business

Hit the Ground Running

There is an old tale according to Nassim Nicholas Taleb in his book, "Skin in the Game", about a conversation between a dog and a wolf [2]. The dog explains to the wolf how good his life is and how he lives in luxury and gets regular meals and is given a bath quite often. The wolf almost becomes jealous until he asks the dog what the collar around his neck is for. When he is told the purpose of the collar, he runs away in horror, wanting no part of the dog's trappings.

The wolf's freedom reminds me of that of the entrepreneur, it's tough out there but hey! you're still your own boss. One of the tough issues the entrepreneur faces is getting funds to build and run his or her business, just like the wolf finds it difficult to get food despite being free.

Hit the Ground Running

Sources of Funds

There are three ways of financing a venture, either through equity or through debt-financing or a combination of equity and debt. Also, funding can come through formal or informal channels. The party that provides equity funds, gets to take part in the ownership of the business, while debt financing is basically a loan that has to be repaid, typically with interest. Informal channels include personal savings, friends and relatives, money lenders and cooperative societies. While formal channels include institutions like commercial banks, development/microfinance banks and other governmental/non-governmental agencies that provide grants or loans to businesses.

This chapter will touch on just a few of these sources of business financing.

Informal Channels

Of course, the most hassle-free source of funding for any business is from **personal savings**, the owner(s) put in money to build and run the business and there is no commitment to any other party asides the taxman. But most times, it's not that easy. There are competing needs for these funds (if available) and it might be smarter to spread the risks, in the event the venture goes south. However, for most entrepreneurs the funds are either not available or not enough to build and run the venture.

Another source of funds could be from **family or friends** and these come with gentler terms, with regards to interest rates and tenures but sometimes with a lot of emotional baggage. Even with the emotional baggage, the gentler terms of payment relieve the entrepreneur from stress of harassment that comes from strangers, when repayment terms are breached. Unfortunately, most entrepreneurs don't have these avenues to tap from and have to rely on other channels.

Other sources of funding that are relatively easy to access are through **moneylenders and cooperative societies**. Although easier to get, compared to formal channels, these parties offer shylock interest rates and very short tenures. I know a fellow that has a job with a monthly salary of about two hundred thousand naira but goes home with approximately seven thousand naira every month because he borrowed from moneylenders and couldn't meet up with the repayments. He was forced to sign away most of his salary to clear out the new sum that had been bloated by these unreasonable monthly interest rates.

Formal Channels

Hit the Ground Running

Moving on to the next source of financing, which are **commercial banks**. These are formal institutions and usually have multiple requirements including collaterals and in Nigeria, the interest rates are usually over twenty percent per annum. This level of interest rate is quite high, but most businesses get funding through this means and its usually a struggle for most to meet up the repayments. I guess that's why wolves are lean.

Micro-finance banks offer a friendlier source of funds to small businesses compared to commercial banks, in the sense that their requirements are not as stringent as the conditions the commercial banks request to give out loans. Also, most state governments channel some funds through micro-finance banks, with the intention to support small businesses. The tenures offered by these institutions are usually shorter and another drawback is that micro-finance banks give out smaller amounts of money as loans to businesses. Of recent, these banks have started asking for security (collateral) in the form of land or buildings, which can make things difficult for smaller businesses. Some state governments have set up their own micro-finance banks and actually give out loans through these banks but unlike in the past, they actively try to recover these loans. Hence, you should not see them as entitlements or grants.

The federal government has several developmental banks and institutions including the government-owned Bank of Industry, which offer another source of funds for Nigerian businesses. Initially designed to support manufacturing, the BOI also supports agriculture, ICT and mining. I'll tell you a story. An acquaintance that runs a manufacturing outfit and was looking for funds to expand her company approached the Bank of Industry. She scheduled an appointment with them and before she had the chance to give her pitch, the BOI official started telling her about her company, the directions to her factory, how many machines she had and how her competitors where doing.

Surprisingly, the BOI does its homework, when it comes to collecting information about Nigerian manufacturers. The BOI typically has longer tenures than micro-finance banks, from around twelve to sixty months and can offer much larger sums of money to businesses. My friend hasn't gotten the loan yet from the BOI but she is hopeful of getting it, once she meets their requirements. You can get more information about BOI from their website - https://www.boi.ng.

There are many other sources of funding out there, including some **government grants and other loan-offering institutions**. It's not always easy to actually get these funds but that should not stop you from trying. Some people just believe it's impossible to get funds from banks or government institutions, while others just don't have the right information. For instance, the CBN insists that micro-finance banks meet up a threshold in terms of financing micro-businesses or these banks could lose their licenses. Hence, it is actually in their interest to give out loans to businesses, as long as you meet their requirements.

One thing is to get a loan, another is to repay that loan, and this is the undoing of a lot of businesspeople. In his book, Shoe Dog, Phil Knight talks of his morning mantra "Pay Nissho first", Nissho being his Japanese bankers[3]. This is very important, as your failure to make payments on time attract charges, which increases your costs of business and worse you could lose your business if the banks get impatient and decide to call in their loans.

By the way, another version of the story I told at the beginning of the chapter, puts a wild ass in the place of the wolf and the wild ass eventually gets eaten by a lion while running free. It's a jungle out there, guys.

Chapter summary/Key takeaways

- Businesses can be financed through equity, debt or a combination of both.
- Sources of funding could also be categorized as informal and formal.

Hit the Ground Running

- Informal sources include personal funds, monies from family and friends and funds from money lenders and informal cooperative societies.
- Formal sources include commercial, micro-finance and government development banks.

In the next chapter we talk about the structure of the organization. I advocate for modern structures that aim to empower employees and encourage better participation. I believe these new flatter structures yield multiple benefits.

Chapter Four – Setting up Your Structure

Hit the Ground Running

In the old days, setting up your organizational structure was a no-brainer. The owner is the chairperson and/or MD-CEO and then there is a General Manager and below departmental heads, then supervisors and so on. Noticed I said 'old days' because this is an antiquated way of thinking and entrepreneurs/SMEs should not fall into the trap of believing this is the only or best way of setting up their organizations.

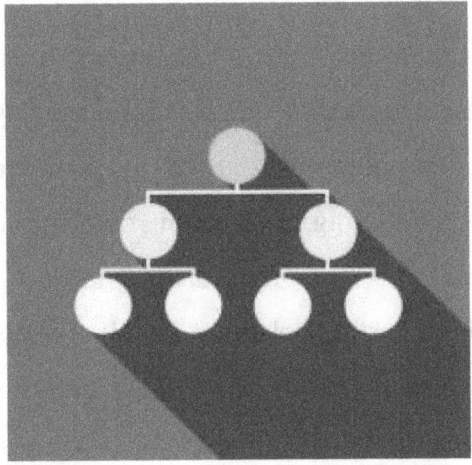

Innovations of today have not left out organizational setups. Management science has offered up new ways of structuring the organization that takes into consideration the need to empower the

45

organizational members, so they can make decisions and speed up the organizational processes and ultimately optimize resources.

The Old Ways Don't Always Work

Management researchers have argued the need to empower workers to various degrees. Empowering employees by involving them in the process of decision-making allows for sharing information, delegation of duties and employee autonomy. This promotes organizational citizenship behavior, which essentially describes when employees go above and beyond what is required of them, on behalf of the organization's success.

Besides, the traditional hierarchical organizational structure does not allow for multi-directional communication flow, limits participation and does not encourage commitment because this structure does not promote that sense of ownership amongst employees. Let's think about it, an employee comes to work every day and is always told what to do and how to go about doing the work, hardly leaving any room for contribution from the employee. I agree it is not always this extreme in most hierarchical structures, but the vertical layers of such systems mostly do not allow for feedback from the bottom to the top. Even when feedback is given, it is often lost or distorted traveling from one layer up to another. However, the information moving from the top to bottom makes use of the official lines of communication through company memos, broadcast emails and message boards, which are often not available for communication flowing the other way around.

Figure 1: Traditional Hierarchical Organizational Structure.

New Structures to Empower

Several strategies are now available to encourage participation and empowerment, these include quality circles/taskforces, team-based structures and other high involvement structures. Quality circles and taskforces are strategies you can adopt when you already have a traditional structure and it's either difficult to change structures or you could utilize this approach as a precursor to changing structures.

     Quality circles usually comprise of a group of individuals from different departments of an organization that volunteer to meet once a week, for some months, to proffer solutions to problems facing the organization. These are problems that usually lack sufficient time or resources, or nobody has responsibility to solve such issues. Quality circles can be rewarded based on the effectiveness of their suggestion and the rewards can be financial or non-financial. Quality circles can come up with suggestions but do not have the power to implement their suggestions that responsibility still lies with the top management. The difference between quality circles and task forces, is that a task force has management personnel as part of the group, while quality circles comprise of individuals outside the top management cadre.

Hit the Ground Running

Work teams (also called self-managing groups, autonomous work groups, semi-autonomous work groups), comprise of groups of employees responsible for delivering a product or service. Work teams are allowed to make operational or tactical decisions such as work scheduling, work methods or procedures and are often allowed to decide on selecting team members and leaders. This approach ensures teams acquire a variety of skills and new knowledge, new feedback systems are provided, and the teams may be rewarded differently based on team performance. The use of work teams increases the influence of organizational members on work methods and how they are rewarded. This could ultimately save costs by allowing individuals perform multiple roles and rewarding them for this, rather than employing additional workers.

Adopting a work team structure usually entails re-training of personnel, physical re-configuration of workspace might also be necessary (although, this will not be necessary if the organization is set up to use work teams from the beginning), as well as deployment of new technology and all these could imply significant costs. In addition, team-members could feel reluctant to share information or knowledge, while senior management could resist sharing power. However, work teams have been reported in resulting in significant improvements in various organizational indices such as performance, job satisfaction and turnover. One of the key reasons why work-teams succeed, and I believe it is a good idea for organizations, is its ability to utilize peer pressure to gain productivity. The pressure from peers is often more influential than from bosses and one's peers know all the tricks when it comes to under-performing on the job, especially in areas where the boss can be fooled more easily.

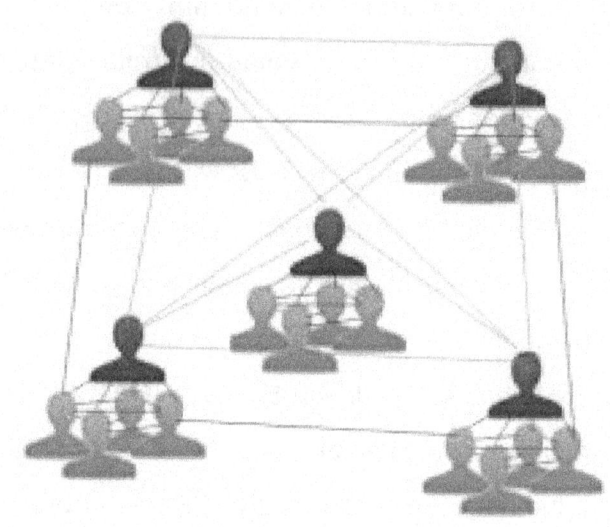

Figure 2: Team Based Organizational Structure.

Work teams can be utilized both in the service and non-service sectors. There have been instances of work-teams set-up in manufacturing plants and oil rig teams. These teams are cross-disciplinary with individuals trained in both operations and maintenance of equipment. This ensures that the team quickly responds to issues such as equipment faults, whilst operations move smoothly. Even in restaurants and other hospitality organizations, such work-teams can be deployed, where chefs can take orders and waiters can give helping hands in the kitchen. The team decides how the work is organized and even how the rewards are distributed. I'm involved in a hospitality outfit and the organization rewards the entire team at the end of the month based on occupancy, this motivates them to not see any activity as 'my job' or 'his job' but everyone chips in to assist the other to ensure customers are happy and return to patronize the establishment. Even the head of the company, also sees herself as part of the team and is willing to chip in to make beds or clean the swimming pool, when whoever is responsible isn't available. The security guys assist in the cleaning, the cleaners are eager to welcome guests and the customers feel well taken care of because of this arrangement.

Chapter summary/Key takeaways

- It is important that entrepreneurs explore new ways of setting up their organizations.

Hit the Ground Running

> Traditional vertical structures inhibit the flow of ideas and stunts employee commitment to the organization.

- Empowerment strategies with regards to the structure of the firm, improves communication and participation; ensures rewards are based on performance; and reduces operational costs.

In the next chapter, we delve into recruitment. How does an entrepreneur go about hiring? What does she look out for and what are the right questions to ask during interview sessions? Let's find out.

Chapter Five - What Comes Through the Door:

Recruiting in Small Businesses

Hit the Ground Running

In the popular story written by Mary Shelley[4], Dr. Frankenstein in a bid to understand and defeat death created what turned out to be monster. His monster left scores dead in its wake and eventually killed not only Frankenstein's beloved wife but Frankenstein, its creator. Talk about a disastrous outcome and this is how hiring can go wrong, although this is an extreme example.

Recruiting is a vital process for any company, as the workforce is the determining ingredient for success or failure in every organization. If hiring goes bad, it usually is costly and small businesses cannot afford too many of such expensive mistakes, hence, it is imperative that the right people are hired most of the time. This makes it even more ironic, when we consider that small businesses hardly put in a thought to the recruitment process. Many entrepreneurs mostly rely on informal methods and taking on friends and family members that are just not right for the positions that need filling. Small businesses owners can hire recruitment consultants but usually can't afford this and have to do it themselves.

Shapes of Holes to Fill

The first step in any hiring process is determining the work that needs to be done i.e. the duties of the particular position you are recruiting for. You have to specifically identify the duties, skills, attributes and experience required and these should be articulated clearly as an initial step. Doing this will help the employer to identify, evaluate and interview candidates. It will also contribute to the job advertisement content, helping to target the right candidates to potentially fill the vacant role or roles.

There are several sources for recruitment, which companies approach to attract a pool of talents. Employee referrals are important and common sources of new recruits. Studies indicate that employees who are referred by other colleagues tend to do a bit better in terms of work performance and this cannot be taken for granted. However, such candidates still need to go through the recruitment process to ensure they are appropriate matches. Other sources are career pages/websites, on-line job boards, internship programs and social media sites. I recently discovered to my surprise that the online store, jiji, is quite popular for job seekers in Nigeria, in addition to the more popular social media sites such as Instagram, Twitter, Facebook, LinkedIn and even Whatsapp updates.

Tools for Treasure Hunting

The next step in recruiting is conducting pre-hiring screening. This involves sifting through the resumes of the candidates or other processes to identify the ones with the appropriate traits, experiences and values. Application tracking software (ATS) can also be used to carry out this process, which could be helpful if you have to go through a huge number of applications. Some organizations also choose to conduct personality and behavioral tests such as the Myer Briggs or other similar tests.

Asking Questions That Reveal

Face-to-face interviews are the most important aspect of the recruitment process, where candidates get the opportunity to sell themselves. During interviews, candidates can also get more information about the company.

Hit the Ground Running

On the flip side, recruiters can glean more about the personalities and levels of qualification of the candidates being considered for the positions during face-to-face interviews. Interviews seek to assess the knowledge, skills, abilities, strengths, weaknesses, interests and goals.

Below is a list of some interview questions that can help reveal these attributes:

- Why did you choose to interview with our company?
- What accomplishments are you most proud of?
- What are your motivations?
- What skills have you developed that would help you prepare for this job?
- Which courses in your major did you like best? Least?
- Have you ever quit a job? Why?
- How do you think your former supervisor would describe your work?
- Do you prefer working under supervision or on your own?

Hit the Ground Running

- Do you prefer a large or small organization and why?
- Tell me about a time when you had to resolve a conflict situation in a group situation?

(Source: American Express Open Forum – Welcome Aboard: Guide to Small Business Hiring [5]).

Doing the Due Diligence

Following the interview sessions, it is essential to carry out background checks. This is an often-skipped process, but many banana skins could have been avoided, if more business owners called referees or former employers of prospective candidates. Some employers also choose to carry out credit and criminal checks.

There are times that a candidate can meet all the criteria for hiring, especially technically and during the interview, the person come across as articulate and composed. However, you might come to discover, as I once did, problems with the behavior or attitude later on.

Hit the Ground Running

I once hired a team member that checked all the boxes at the time of recruitment, but we later discovered that this person was short-tempered and was always ready to resolve to fisticuffs when provoked. We eventually had to make the tough and expensive decision to fire the employee. If we had carried out some background checks, we probably could have learnt of this side of the recruit, before we made the final decision.

You're Hired! What's Next?

The process doesn't end after the interviews and selection of candidates. Welcoming new employees is a crucial step. This helps them feel at home and generally bed-in properly. Orientation programs can be organized, systems should be set up to monitor, coach and map career goals.

Finally, employers hiring for the first time might also need to pay attention to the following requirements (they would probably need to consult a lawyer or an accountant):

Hit the Ground Running

- Get employer identification number from the internal revenue service.
- Pay taxes and set up records for withholding taxes.
- Carry workers compensation insurance.

Chapter Summary/Key Takeaways

- Write down the skills and attributes you desire from your new hires.
- You can prune down the number of potential candidates by carrying out pre-hiring screening.
- Select the write questions to ask during the interview sessions to help you identify the right fit for the positions.
- Carry out your due diligence after interviewing by calling references and carrying out background checks.

Hit the Ground Running

Bibliography

1. Malik, K. A. (2014), "Economic Viability of Petroleum Projects", International Petroleum Management Program, Module 1-Part 1.
2. Taleb, N. N. (2018), "Skin in the Game: Hidden Asymmetries in Daily Life", Penguin.
3. Knight, P. (2016), "Shoe Dog: A Memoir by the Creator of Nike", Simon & Schuster, London.
4. Varoufakis, Y. (2017), "Talking to My Daughter about the Economy", Vintage, London.
5. SmartBrief Media Services, "Welcome Aboard: Guide to Small Business Hiring", American Express Open Forum.
6. Kotler, P. and Keller, K. L. (2009), "Marketing Management", 13th Edition, Pearson Prentice Hall, London.
7. Bank of Industry, (2020), Home page, https://www.boi.ng.

8. SmartBrief Media Services, (2013), "Welcome Aboard: Guide to Small Business Hiring", American Express Open Forum, http://www.leapros.com/assets/downloads/AmexHiring_final.pdf.

9. Lawler III, E. E. (1988), "Choosing an Involvement Strategy", *Academy of Management Executive*, **2**(3), pp.197-204.

10. Lawler III, Edward E. and Susan A. MOHRMAN, (1987), "Quality Circles: After the Honeymoon", *Organizational Dynamics*. **15**(4), pp.42-54.

11. Ake, U. (2019), "Improving Organizational Commitment in the Nigerian Service Industry", Doctor of Business Administration Thesis, University of Liverpool.

12. Ake, U. (2009), "Business Plan: Afri Sun Electricity Generating Company", Module Paper Submitted for the Entrepreneurship Module, University of Liverpool.

APPENDIX: Sample Business Plan

Business Plan

Afri Sun Electricity Generating Company

By

Ukadike Ake

Hit the Ground Running

Initial Situational Analysis

1.1 Vision and Strategy Statement

The company aims to alleviate the problem of insufficient electricity in Nigeria by generating electricity using gas turbines fueled by abundant natural gas resources.

1.2 The Problem / Need

Nigeria is currently generating about 2500Megawatts of electric power which is by far below sufficient levels for a population of one hundred and forty million (140,000,000) people, in fact this figure is not enough to meet the entire needs of its capital city Abuja. The government estimates that it would need up to 100,000 megawatts to meet its desire of being an industrialized nation and this would require an investment of about $85 billion (BBC website; 2008).

To achieve this would require partnership from the private sector as well and the government is desperate for participation from the private sector. The country's electricity regulatory body lists the encouragement of private sector participation in the electricity market as one of its goals (NERC website; 2009). Also, the government has spent up to $10 billion in the last ten years with little results and recently set up an Infrastructure Concession Regulatory Commission to drive private investment in infrastructure including electricity provision (Nigerian Tribune newspaper website; 2009).

1.3 The Opportunity

Nigeria is reported to account for a total of 3% of the world's natural gas reserves and is amongst the top ten countries with the largest natural gas reserves (Eni world oil and gas review 2008; 2009). However, poor government practices/policies and lack of investment in power generation through harnessing of gas has been the reason why this opportunity has not been exploited and a lot of associated gas that is produced alongside crude oil is being flared into the atmosphere. The Nigerian government has given a deadline of 2010 for all oil producing companies to put an end to gas flaring by threatening sanctions and also is investing in the treatment of the gas for domestic and export purposes (un.org).

1.4 Consumer Situation on Ground

Currently, most of the country's residents have to rely on generating sets run by petrol or diesel for electric power consumption and these end up costing three times the normal cost of electricity from the national power supply network. In addition to the high costs, these generating plants pose safety risks and sources of pollution; the potential for fire accidents is greater using these generators; and pollution of the air from their exhaust pipes and the noise pollution because of the proximity to the living houses is rife with these generating sets.

Also, most of the country's industries are crumbling under the lack of electricity power infrastructure because the high costs of running independent generating plants and competition from foreign manufacturers makes it difficult to raise prices of products to offset the additional power costs. In recent months, many companies have either folded up business or relocated to nearby countries; last year the French tyre manufacturing company, Michelin, decided to take its West African plant to neighboring country, Ghana, consequently resulting in huge job and revenue losses for the Nigerian economy.

Hit the Ground Running

Management Plan

2.1 Introduction

According to Ron Bloom of PodShow, "the first ten or twenty people in your organization put a DNA stamp on the organization", hence it is vital that these set of people will add value and help the company to achieve its vision; and they would most likely include the founder(s), investing partners and the top management team.

The management plan section aims to display that; the business is organized in a manner that will guarantee success; the management team possesses the right skills and qualities; and necessary supporting and corporate governance structures are in place.

2.2 Founder and Joint Venture Partners

The directors of Afri-Sun will include representatives of the founding company, Ake Technologies and the joint venture partners which

Hit the Ground Running

include ABC Petroleum Producing Company of Nigeria and the Nigerian Petroleum Company. The founding company is a young innovative company with experience in electrical power installation and its owner, Ukadike Ake, has worked in the energy sector for seven years as an engineer and holds an MBA degree from the University of Liverpool, United Kingdom. He has gone through training in Crafting and Executing Strategy; Marketing; Financial and Operations Management; and Entrepreneurship. The experience he lacks he hopes to make up for in knowledge and a vast network of business contacts and also in assembling a formidable management team that will bring in skills from different disciplines.

The ABC Petroleum Producing Company of Nigeria is a subsidiary of the multinational energy company Xetra-ABC Company based in Italy which is into exploration and production of petroleum and natural gas; refining and distribution of petroleum products; electricity generation; and construction of plants and oil field installations. The company brings in a wealth of experience from the energy business especially electricity generation and supply but most importantly, the company will provide the feed gas for the gas turbine plant at slightly less than market prices. Also, the company will provide part of the capital to finance the project.

The Nigerian Petroleum Company is the national oil company (NOC) of the country; it also brings in a wealth of experience from the energy sector and will represent an investment stakeholder for the Nigerian government in the venture. The company will provide needed leverage and insight into the Nigerian business environment and also provide contacts to allow for easier acquisition of the licenses required for the project. Also, the company will ensure that there is the desired local content participation in a project of this magnitude while also contributing in the financing of the project.

2.3 Management Team

Hit the Ground Running

The Management team will be comprised of the Chief Executive Officer, Chief Financial Officer, Chief Operations Officer and the heads of Legal Affairs, Marketing, Strategies and Development, Internal Audit, and Corporate Affairs and Governance. The organizational chart can be found in the appendix section of this management plan.

The Chief Executive Officer (CEO) will head the management team and he or she will be responsible for the day to day running of the company and to ensure its success. The CEO is charged with the overall responsibility of crafting and executing strategy which he/she carries out in conjunction with the rest of the company. The chief executive officer must manage both human and non-human resources to meet the objectives of the company and ensure its profitability both in the long-term and short-term periods in a sustainable and ethical manner.

The Chief Financial Officer (CFO) is responsible for both the financial and management accounting functions of the company which is vital for decision-making; he or she is responsible in advising the CEO and the board on financial matters concerning the company. Also, it is the CFO's overall responsibility to prepare and provide accounting statements and reports for both internal and external consumption as regards to the company. The CFO will advise on the viability of the project and also carry out cost control and budgetary functions; the CFO is also responsible in contributing to the strategy at the top management end of the company.

The Chief Operating Officer is responsible in carrying out the core operations of the company which in this case is generating of electricity to be sold to the final consumers which are the country's citizens and industries through the National Power/Utility Company. The COO is in charge of the technical (operations, maintenance and safety) and non-technical aspects such as logistics and human resources functions that will result in the effective delivery of the company's products. Directly functioning under the chief operating officer are the plant superintendent- who oversees the electricity generating plant; and the senior operations engineer- who is responsible for interfacing with the clients and the government regulators of the electricity sector. The COO is responsible for strategy at the operational level and must work with other top management functionaries to achieve the company's objectives.

Marketing Plan

3.1 Target Markets

- The national utility company

- Regional or state governments

- Industrial and commercial users

- Residential consumers.

Hit the Ground Running

3.2 Geographics

The target region for the company's product is the Niger Delta region of Nigeria with a population of 20 million people and a population growth rate of 2.9% (National Population Commission; 2003). This area is also the centre of the petroleum industry with all the major producing and servicing companies having their presence in the area as well as numerous industrial and manufacturing complexes. Due to the activities of the oil and gas industry, there has been a lot of migration from other parts of the country and expatriate staff from all over the world.

3.3 Market Trends

Since the 1990s, countries throughout Africa started to unbundle the task of power generation from state owned utility companies by privatizing the power sector because of the inefficient handling by the utility companies and unavailability of funds from the governments. Private companies invested in the energy sector by building Independent Power Plants (IPPs) and several players have entered the power generation business in Nigeria including multinational companies and regional governments with the purpose of selling the electricity generated to utility companies such as the Power Holding Company of Nigeria (PHCN).

Eni, through its Nigerian subsidiary in conjunction with PhillipsConoco and the Nigerian National Petroleum Company commissioned a 450MW power plant in 2005 in Okpai, while Shell Petroleum Nigeria started operations in its own 650MW IPP in 2008 in Afam; these plants are situated in the Niger Delta area because of the proximity to natural gas supply but supply directly to the national grid that is transmitted throughout the country.

The Federal Government through its National Integrated Power Project hopes to achieve an additional 6000 MW by construction six new power plants across the country by the end of 2009, also state governments like Rivers, Lagos and Akwa Ibom states have also invested in Independent Power Plants of their own.

3.4 Market Growth

Currently the entire country is generating about 2500 MW of electricity and by the end of 2010 the Nigerian government hopes that investments from both the government and the private sector would boost the supply of electricity to 15,000 MW (Gratwick & Eberhard; 2007). The government believes however that to become an industrialized nation, a capacity of a 100,000 MW generation is needed (BBC website; 2008).

The federal government is in charge of energy distribution, but plans are being made to allow state governments to purchase and distribute electricity on their own.

3.5 Competition

The company faces competition from both direct and indirect competitors, its direct competitors are other companies that generate and supply electricity to the state utility company (PHCN) while indirect competitors provide alternative sources of electricity directly to the ultimate consumers.

The direct competitors include the federal government owned power plants powered by both natural gas and hydro-dams (Shiroro and Kainji dams); privately owned power plants owned by multinationals like RoyalDutch Shell (Afam IPP) and Eni (Okpai IPP); power plants owned by regional state governments like Rivers State (Omoku and Trans-Amadi Gas Turbines) and Akwa-Ibom State (Ibom Power Project); and emerging entrants like Chevron and other indigenous firms.

Whereas the indirect competitions come through low capacity power generating devices like fuel (petrol or diesel) generating sets and solar panels;

that are purchased by the final consumers and installed in their premises and not through any utility company.

3.6 Pricing Strategy

The company intends to build its pricing strategy and objectives around high quality and reliability of services it provides its customers rather than just offering cheapest prices. The company intends to provide steady and reliable electricity supply as well as keeping the varying needs of its clients at the heart of its services. However, in Nigeria, electricity prices are monitored and regulated by the Nigerian Electricity Regulatory Commission (NERC) which is responsible for ensuring that pricing is fair and profitable (NERC website; 2009); and the company intends to adhere to the country's regulations.

3.7 Marketing Organization

The marketing functions will be carried out by the marketing department headed by the Chief Marketing Officer and this department would be responsible for the brand strategy, marketing research, pricing strategy and also public relations. The department would also outsource some activities to external marketing firms and consultants. Marketing channels would include print, media, the internet and through sponsorship of philanthropic events.

Financial Plan

4.1 Introduction

The financial plan presents the intention of the company in ensuring success through sound financial actions and policies. The plan explains the accounting role of the company, how the management intends to finance the venture and also pro-forma balance sheet and profit & loss statement. In order to ensure full and accurate disclosure the company intends to use up-to-date accounting software, qualified personnel and also external auditors.

4.2 Accounting System

The accounting function in the company will be directly under the control of the Chief Financial Officer (CFO) who will be responsible for both financial and management accounting functions and reporting. Accounting software to be deployed will be SAP and also external auditors will be utilized to ensure the veracity of reports presented as this is stipulated by law.

4.3 Underlying Assumptions

- All the energy produced by Afri-Sun will be purchased by the National Electricity Utility Company or the regional utility company.

- The price of energy supplied will fluctuate using the OECD (Organization for Economic Cooperation and Development) total consumer price index.
- Sales invoices are to be paid not more than three months after supply of energy.
- Start-up charges will apply for additional start-ups caused by failure in clients receiving equipment.

4.4 Financing the Venture

The decisions made by management in sourcing funds needed are crucial in every organization as this affects both the short-term and long-term financial performance and organizational motivation. Sources of finance can either be external or internal; external sources include sales of shares (ordinary and preference), loans, bank overdraft and invoice discounting; while internal sources include retained profits, reduction in inventory levels and delayed payment of trade payables.

Hit the Ground Running

To carry out the project of setting up and running the power plant, Afri-Sun intends to raise money through bank loans and also obtain funds from the joint venture partners as equity investment and also a policy of tight credit control will be carried out by the management.

At start-up the company intends to have a financial gearing ratio of 36 percent which is not too significant for a venture of this size.

4.5 *Profitability*

For the first six months the projected return of capital employed (ROCE) is only 17.3 percent but this is understandable and will improve as the long-term loans are paid up.

However, the net profit margin for the initial six months is projected at 59 percent which is a

Hit the Ground Running

healthy figure; also, the company intends to break-even in the first five years of operation.

$$ROCE = \frac{\text{Net profit before interest and tax}}{\text{Share capital+ Long term loans}} \times 100 = 617/3566.85 \times 100 = 17.3\%$$

$$\text{Net Profit Margin} = \frac{\text{Net profit before interest and tax}}{\text{Sales revenue}} \times 100 = 617/1050 \times 100 = 59\%$$

BREAK-EVEN ANALYSIS

Fixed costs = $450 million

Sales revenue per unit = $13/kW/month

Variable cost per unit = $10/kW/month

No. of units at Break-even point = Fixed cost/ (Sales revenue per unit − Variable cost per unit)

= 450,000,000/ (10-3) kW/month

= 150,000 kW/month

Conclusion

The project of building an electricity generating power plant in Nigeria presents an opportunity for a potentially profitable venture in a country in desperate need of infrastructural investments and an abundance of cheap natural gas.

Also, the experience and financial muscle of the joint venture partners are strengths that would surely bring benefits to the venture in terms of stability and avoiding costly mistakes while achieving operational excellence.

However, the weaknesses of the company include the dependence on additional funding from financial institutions and absence of multiple clients outside the government utility companies.

Also, external threats that confront the company are the volatile and potentially violent nature of the Niger Delta region of Nigeria due to aggrieved communities as regards crude oil and natural gas exploration in the area; and also the swampy nature of the terrain in the Niger Delta could pose logistics problems for the company.

In spite of the difficulties, the company can adopt the right operational strategy to take advantage of the opportunities and avoid problems posed by threats mentioned. The company's strategy is a sustainable one because it strongly considers the environment and relationship with its host communities; and with proper planning and a highly qualified management team the other logistics and operational challenges can be adequately tackled.

Acknowledgments

My profound gratitude goes to so many people that made this book possible, if I fail to mention you, please forgive me.

I would like to thank all those that contributed to the research for this book: Uloma Diriyai, Ok Chike, Isioma, Boma Obuforibo Jr., Phillip Beke and Ozu Ake.

I also am indebted to Ernest Umeike for the grammar advice and to Gerald Ogbonna for allowing me write articles on entrepreneurship for our class alumni magazine.

Charles Okebunnor, special thanks to you. You gave me the push, when I almost gave up.

About the Author

The author, Ukadike Ake, is a serial entrepreneur with forays into various sectors including entertainment, construction, equipment leasing, real estate and hospitality, all within a span of 25 years. He has experiences being an employee and an employer of labour.

Ukadike Ake holds degrees in Engineering and Business Administration/Management including a Doctorate in Business Administration from the University of Liverpool. He has also conducted several training workshops in business skills including topics in business communications, managing change, team building and supervision.

He currently resides in Port Harcourt, Nigeria with his wife and kids. He's an avid golfer and passionately follows football and basketball.

www.ingramcontent.com/pod-product-compliance
Lightning Source LLC
Chambersburg PA
CBHW050246220526
45465CB00002B/568